FIREFIGHTER

IN TRAINING

⚠️ **REMEMBER**

STAY SAFE! FIREFIGHTING IS DANGEROUS.

ONLY TRAINED ADULT FIREFIGHTERS SHOULD EVER TRY TO PUT OUT A FIRE OR TACKLE AN EMERGENCY.

←--- Can you find me on every page?

KINGFISHER

FIREFIGHTER ACADEMY

TRAINING PROGRAMME

FIRE ACADEMY

FIREFIGHTER

IN TRAINING

9018176249

FIRE ACADEMY

STUDENT PASS

Name ....

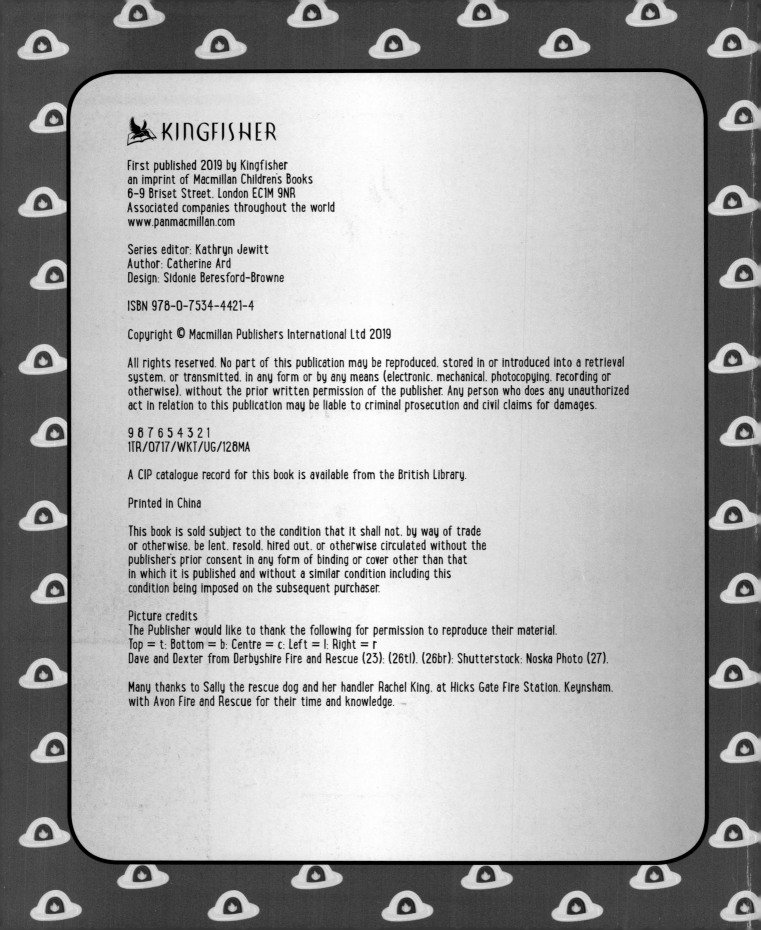

KINGFISHER

First published 2019 by Kingfisher
an imprint of Macmillan Children's Books
6-9 Briset Street, London EC1M 9NR
Associated companies throughout the world
www.panmacmillan.com

Series editor: Kathryn Jewitt
Author: Catherine Ard
Design: Sidonie Beresford-Browne

ISBN 978-0-7534-4421-4

9 8 7 6 5 4 3 2 1
1TR/0717/WKT/UG/128MA

A CIP catalogue record for this book is available from the British Library.

Printed in China

Picture credits
The Publisher would like to thank the following for permission to reproduce their material.
Top = t; Bottom = b; Centre = c; Left = l; Right = r
Dave and Dexter from Derbyshire Fire and Rescue (23); (26tl); (26br); Shutterstock: Noska Photo (27).

Many thanks to Sally the rescue dog and her handler Rachel King, at Hicks Gate Fire Station, Keynsham, with Avon Fire and Rescue for their time and knowledge.

THEORY

PRACTICAL

THEORY pages are full of important information that you need to know.

PRACTICAL pages have a task to do or a firefighting skill to acquire. Tick each page when you have completed that part of your training.

WHAT DO FIREFIGHTERS DO?

Firefighters put out fires and risk their lives to save people, but there's much more to the job than that. Check out all the important work that a firefighter has to do.

1. PREVENT

Firefighters want to stop fires from starting. They visit homes, schools and work places to teach people about fire safety. They also check that buildings are not in danger of catching fire.

2. PROTECT

If a fire starts, firefighters want people to get out safely. They fit smoke alarms in homes. The alarms beep loudly when a fire starts. They also check restaurants, offices and schools to make sure they are prepared for a fire.

ACTIVITY

Can you spot all these pieces of firefighting equipment on these pages?

3. RESCUE

Firefighters put out fires in buildings, in vehicles and out in the open. They also race to road accidents and emergencies and rescue people and animals who are trapped or in danger.

4. MAKE SAFE

Firefighters remove dangers from roads, such as fallen trees and oil or petrol spills in the road. They close roads and keep people away from the scene of accidents. They have to clear up after fires, too.

THEORY NO: 1
tick here
APPROVED

FIRE FACT FILE

Before you start your training, you need to know more about the flames and fire you'll be working with. Discover how dangerous fire can be, how it starts and how it can be stopped.

🔥 QUICK FIRE FACTS

FAST! It only takes 30 seconds for a flame to turn into a fire.

HOT! The air inside a burning room can be 300°C (600°F). That's hotter than a very hot oven.

DARK! Fires make thick, black smoke and poisonous gases fill the air.

⚠️ BE SAFE!

NEVER PLAY WITH OR LEAVE UNATTENDED . . .

 ⭕ matches or lighters

 ⭕ lit candles

 ⭕ cookers and hobs

 ⭕ the fireplace or heaters

 ⭕ lit barbecues

Fire is useful for heating our homes and cooking our food, but it can be dangerous, too. Leave the things below for an adult to look after.

NEVER TOUCH. . .

 ⭕ loose wires

 ⭕ faulty sockets

THEORY NO: 2
⭕ ✓ tick here
APPROVED

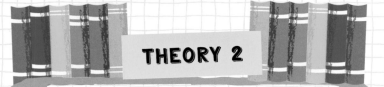

OXYGEN
This is the gas in the air that we breathe.

WHAT MAKES FIRE?
Three things are needed for a fire to start burning – oxygen, heat and fuel. This is called a 'fire triangle'.

Oxygen

Heat

Fuel

FUEL
Anything that burns, such as wood, paper, plastic or fabric.

HEAT
This is anything with a flame or that gives off heat.

WHAT STOPS FIRE?
To stop a fire in its tracks, take away one thing from the fire triangle. Which thing is being taken away in each of the examples below – oxygen, heat or fuel?

ACTIVITY

Soak the hot flames with cold water or foam.

Cover the flames with something, like a thick blanket.

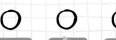

Clear away plants and trees to stop forest fires spreading.

PRACTICAL 1

TRAINING TIME

So you want to be a firefighter? Are you strong, calm and fearless? Got a good head for heights and love working in a team? Then welcome to fire school! Your training starts here.

First up, it's hose training. It takes two firefighters to hold a gushing hose. Twist the nozzle to control the spray. You'll learn to unroll and roll up hoses, too.

START

HOSE TROUBLE

The hoses have got tangled up — can you help find which hose leads to which firefighter?

You'll be taught how to raise a long ladder and climb safely to the top.

START

🔥 **QUICK FIRE FACT**

Up to 350 litres of water shoot out of a fire hose every minute – that's enough to fill a big bathtub!

FIREFIGHTER KIT

Congratulations! You passed your training with top marks. Collect your new kit and try it on for size.

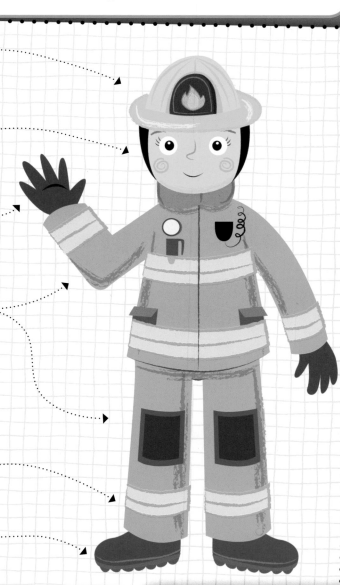

HELMET protects you from falling objects.

FLASH HOOD goes under the helmet to cover your neck and ears.

GLOVES protect your hands from hot surfaces and sharp objects.

TROUSERS AND JACKET are made from special, thick material that protects you from heat and flames.

REFLECTIVE STRIPES help other firefighters see you in the dark.

HEAVY BOOTS stop your feet from burning and protect them from hard objects.

✳ ✳ TRAINEE TIP
A firefighter's clothing is often called 'turnouts' or 'bunker gear'.

BREATHING APPARATUS

A mask and air tank allow you to breathe clean air inside a hot, smoky building.

GAS-TIGHT SUIT

This suit is worn on top of all of the other kit if there are dangerous chemicals at an incident.

Spot the four differences between the two pictures.

ACTIVITY

USEFUL TOOLS

Can you spot them all?

TORCH
to see in the dark

AXE
to break down doors

RADIO
to speak to other firefighters

PRACTICAL NO: 2

tick here

APPROVED

THE FIRE STATION

This is the fire station where you will complete your training. Take a tour around and find out what happens where.

START

1 The fire engines are parked in the big garage.

2 Your kit hangs near the engine, ready to put on.

3 You will study new firefighting skills in the training room.

4 Everyone cooks and eats together in the kitchen.

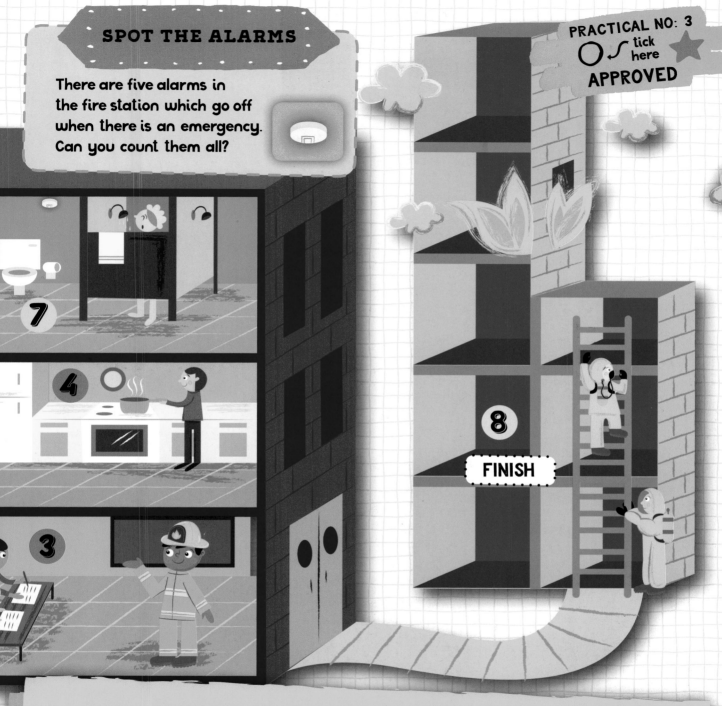

SPOT THE ALARMS

There are five alarms in the fire station which go off when there is an emergency. Can you count them all?

FINISH

5 The control room is where all the information about emergencies comes in.

6 Work out in the gym for an hour a day to stay firefighter-fit!

7 You will need to wash away the soot after a fire emergency.

8 Many fire stations have buildings where firefighters can practise using their breathing apparatus in special smoke-filled rooms.

AWESOME ENGINE

Fire engines are called out to all sorts of emergencies, from blazes to car crashes. Check out the important kit they carry and find out where you will be sitting.

Siren and flashing lights

Traffic cones to keep the road clear

Ladders are carried on the roof

Hoses are neatly rolled away

Seats for the driver and five firefighters in the cab

Fan to clear smoke out of a building

Fire extinguishers for putting out small fires

Help the firefighter put the equipment away. Where does each thing belong?

○ traffic cone ○ hose

○ hammer ○ fire extinguisher

✱✱ TRAINEE TIP
The fire engine is sometimes called 'the appliance'.

First-aid kit and stretcher

THE PUMP
A big tank inside the fire engine carries enough water to put out a small fire. Hoses are fixed on at the back of the engine and a pump pushes the water so that it shoots out really fast.

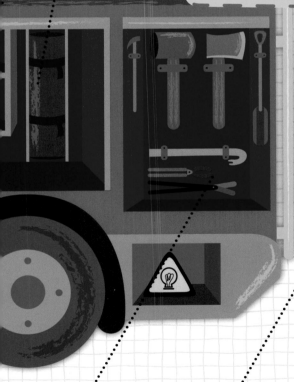

Tools for breaking down doors and for beating out fires

Warning lights for night-time emergencies

🔥 QUICK FIRE FACT
A fire engine weighs more than 12 cars, but it can still speed along at 112 kph!

A FIREFIGHTER'S DAY

TRAINEE TIP

A team of firefighters is called a 'watch'. Each watch is often named after a colour – you are in Blue Watch.

It's your first day on the job! The fire station is ready for action 24 hours a day and there's always plenty to do. Hurry – it's time to report for duty!

9:00am

ROLL CALL

Line up with the rest of your team. The firefighter in charge will give you your jobs for the day.

9:30am

CHECKS

Inspect, clean and tidy the equipment on the fire engine so that everything is ready for the next emergency.

10:00am

TRAINING

Firefighters practise their skills every day. Today you have to wriggle through tight spaces with all your gear on!

12:00pm

LUNCH

Tomato soup with the rest of the crew. It's hot, hot, hot!

CALL OUT

2:30pm

Rescue two people who are stuck in a lift at a shopping centre. Heave!

WORKOUT

4:00pm

Hit the fire station gym and work up a sweat.

WRITE REPORT

5:00pm

Write up everything that happened at the lift rescue.

CLEAN UP

6:30pm

Have dinner, then get the station clean and tidy, ready for the next shift.

BEDTIME

9:00pm

Fall into your bed at the fire station. What a day! Hopefully it will be a quiet night...

ACTIVITY

PRACTICAL NO: 4

⬤ ↶ tick here

APPROVED

Practise your report-writing skills! Write up a report of what you did today.

EMERGENCY!

Ding-aling-aling-aling! Wake up! When an emergency call comes in late at night, you have to be ready for action.

ACTIVITY

Oh dear! This incident report is in a muddle! Can you work out the real order in which everything happened?

We put on our protective gear and raced to the engine.

Someone smelt smoke. They called 999 and told the operator there was a fire in a neighbour's house.

TRAINEE TIP

Leave your boots inside your trousers so that you can pull them on quickly.

Information about the emergency arrived at the fire station's control room.

The engine sped through the dark streets. The lights were flashing and the siren was blaring in traffic.

We arrived at the scene and saw smoke coming from a downstairs window.

The driver talked to the control centre on the radio to get more information about the emergency.

We entered the house, but only found a piece of toast that had been left under the grill. Everyone was safe.

Cars heard the siren and moved out of the way to let the fire engine speed past.

QUICK FIRE FACT

Firefighters have 60 seconds to put on their kit and get in the fire engine. Can you get dressed in one minute?

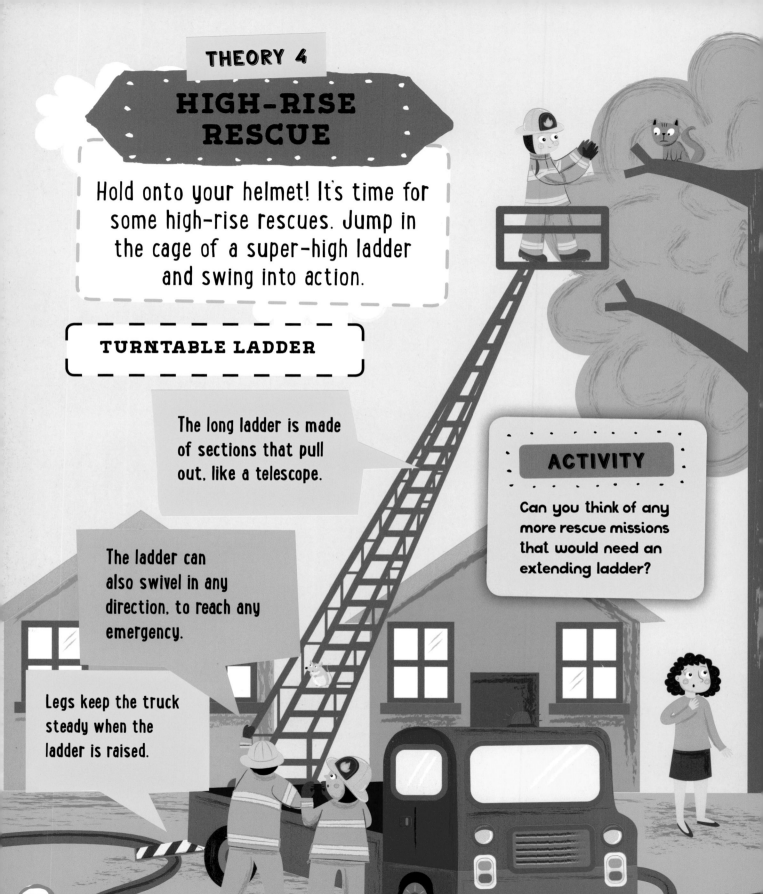

THEORY 4

HIGH-RISE RESCUE

Hold onto your helmet! It's time for some high-rise rescues. Jump in the cage of a super-high ladder and swing into action.

TURNTABLE LADDER

The long ladder is made of sections that pull out, like a telescope.

The ladder can also swivel in any direction, to reach any emergency.

Legs keep the truck steady when the ladder is raised.

ACTIVITY

Can you think of any more rescue missions that would need an extending ladder?

QUICK FIRE FACT

The tallest aerial ladder platforms can reach to the very top of a 15-storey skyscraper!

AERIAL LADDER PLATFORM

The driver uses controls to move the ladder and work the water spray.

Firefighters in the cage spray the fire with water and rescue trapped people.

This bendy ladder can reach up and over things to fight fires from above.

Water is pumped up to the top of the ladder from the truck below.

THEORY NO: 4
tick here
APPROVED

FIRE AND SMOKE

Firefighters practise fire rescues regularly, so prepare for a tricky training day. You are about to enter a smoke-filled building and get someone out safely.

Can you spot which firefighter needs their oxygen tank topping up before the training begins?

Training			12.52
AMY			100%
JACK			88%
LUKE			100%

RESCUE CHECKLIST

It's hard to see in the thick smoke. Follow these steps to guide you from the START to the FINISH.

- ◯ Put on your **BREATHING APPARATUS** (called B.A.) so you can breathe fresh air.

- ◯ Sign the **B.A. BOARD** before you go into the building.

- ◯ Hold the **LINE** and follow the others.

- ◯ Use the **THERMAL IMAGING CAMERA** to find the person in the thick smoke.

- ◯ **CARRY** the person to safety, using the line to guide you.

- ◯ Give the rescued person some **OXYGEN**.

B.A. BOARD

Timers on the board show how much air each firefighter has in their breathing tank. An alarm sounds when their air is getting low.

BREATHING APPARATUS

START

LINE

The firefighter at the front trails a line behind them to guide the others, and to help everyone find their way back out.

THERMAL IMAGING CAMERA

Warm bodies show up on the screen of this special camera. It shows the hottest part of the fire, too.

CARRY

Locate the person and help them to safety.

OXYGEN

A mask connected to a tank of breathing gas, called oxygen, helps people recover from breathing in smoke.

FINISH

PRACTICAL NO: 6

tick here

APPROVED

25

HAIRY HEROES

Today you will be hanging out with a four-legged fire worker. His super sense of smell can help firefighters to search for clues and save lives.

SUPER SNIFFER

Meet Dexter, the fire investigation dog. He is bursting with energy, and great at following smells.

He lives with his handler and travels to work in a special van. He does lots of training and practises his sniffing skills every day.

○ A game of fetch-the-ball is the perfect reward for a job well done.

Once a blaze has been put out, Dexter can search for clues. He is trained to sniff out liquids, such as petrol, that are used to start fires on purpose.

SEARCH AND RESCUE

Some dogs are trained to search for survivors. They can squeeze into tiny spaces in collapsed buildings. When they find someone, they bark to alert their handler.

ACTIVITY

Test your nose! Ask a friend to find some smelly things. Put on a blindfold and sniff each one. Can you guess what they are?

CANINE KIT

○ The harness has torches built in for working in the dark.

○ A body suit helps to keep the dog safe from harmful chemicals.

○ Fire boots protect paws from hot floors and sharp objects.

GOING UP

Working up high is no problem for canine fire crew. They hitch a ride on a ladder or are clipped into a harness and pulled up by rope.

THEORY NO: 5

○ lick here

APPROVED

ROPE RESCUES

A firefighter's life is full of ups and downs. You need a good head for heights for these tricky rescues, so hold on tight!

DOWN A WELL
A walker has fallen down an old well and broken his leg. It's going to take teamwork to bring him up to safety.

1 A pulley is set up over the hole.

2 A tube is dropped down to take fresh air to the bottom.

3 Firefighters are lowered down.

4 The walker is carefully strapped onto a stretcher and pulled up to safety.

5 The team at the top guide the stretcher to stop it swinging.

TRAINEE TIP

A pulley is a wheel with a groove for a rope to pass through. It is often used by firefighters to lift or lower heavy objects.

OFF A CLIFF

A boy is clinging to a cliff ledge. It's all hands to the rescue!

1 Special poles are set up so the rope can be lowered smoothly over the edge.

2 The team lower the rescuer over the edge.

3 The leader tells them when to stop lowering.

ACTIVITY

Which three things would you need for a rope rescue?

- ⚪ hose
- ⚪ hard hat
- ⚪ axe
- ⚪ ropes
- ⚪ harness

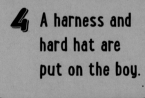

4 A harness and hard hat are put on the boy.

5 The boy and the rescuer are lowered safely to the bottom.

29

ROAD TRAFFIC ACCIDENT

A call-out to a car crash is always a tough job. Practise your skills at this training day, ready for the real thing.

Cut the roof off the car to free the passengers trapped inside. These giant tools slice straight through metal.

Keep the passengers calm and give them first aid until the ambulance arrives.

ACTIVITY

Can you spot these things at the accident training day?

- ○ stretcher
- ○ dangerous chemicals sign
- ○ traffic cone
- ○ rescue tool
- ○ foam fire extinguisher

QUICK FIRE FACT

On training days, firefighters practise by rescuing dummies and treating people with pretend injuries.

If a dangerous chemical is spilt, you need to wear a protective suit to clear it up.

Burning oil or petrol needs to be sprayed with special foam, which smothers the flames.

Block the road to stop people from getting too close.

PRACTICAL NO: 7
○ tick here
APPROVED

OUT AND ABOUT

Firefighting is also about stopping fires from ever starting. Hop in the fire engine and head into town. People need your help to stay safe at home, school and work.

Follow the roads to find all of the buildings.

EXIT

2 THE BAKERY

Problem: the fire extinguishers are covered in bakers' aprons.

1 THE RESTAURANT

Problem: piles of rubbish that could catch fire are blocking the way out.

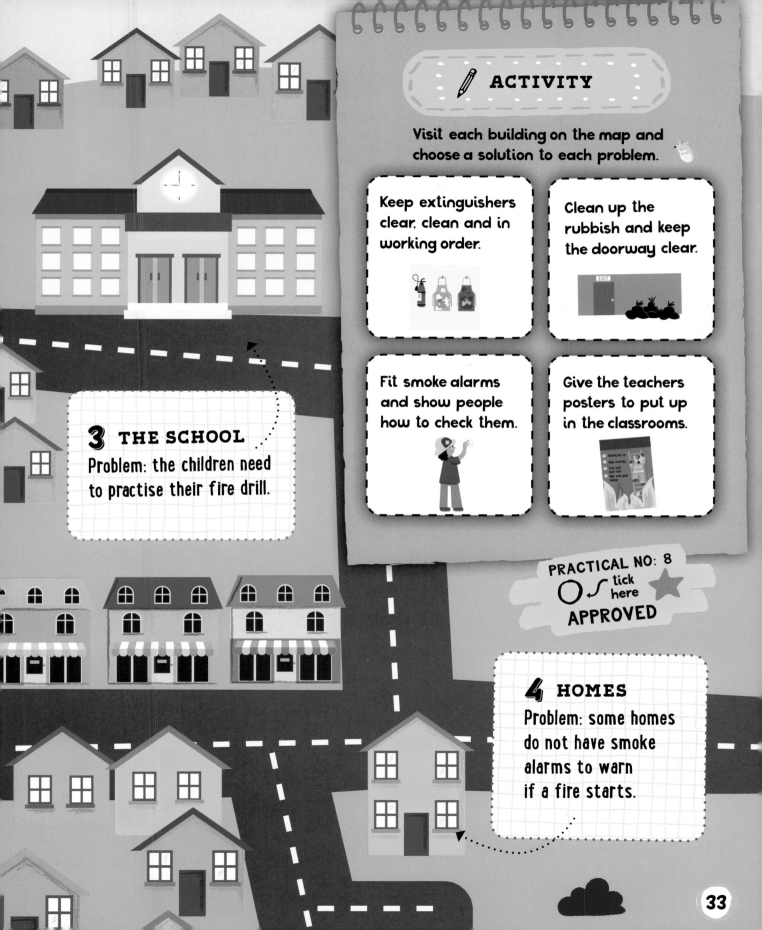

✏️ ACTIVITY

Visit each building on the map and choose a solution to each problem.

Keep extinguishers clear, clean and in working order.

Clean up the rubbish and keep the doorway clear.

Fit smoke alarms and show people how to check them.

Give the teachers posters to put up in the classrooms.

3 THE SCHOOL
Problem: the children need to practise their fire drill.

PRACTICAL NO: 8
○ tick here
APPROVED

4 HOMES
Problem: some homes do not have smoke alarms to warn if a fire starts.

HOUSE OF HORRORS

Carry out a safety inspection at this house. There are fire dangers to find in every room.

Can you spot these things? Tick the box when you find each one.

○ **electric sockets** with too many plugs can catch fire.

○ **cooking** should not be left unwatched.

○ **smoke alarms** should be checked to make sure they are working.

○ **open fires** should have a guard around them.

○ **candles** can set fire to things around them.

○ **heaters** should not be covered by things that can catch fire.

SITTING ROOM

This vehicle has caterpillar treads instead of wheels. It can roll over anything from snow and mud to sinking sand.

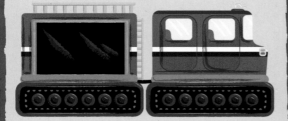

Good for: rescues and fire fighting in mountains and hard-to-reach places.
Kit on board: search lights, ladders and hoses.
Firefighters on board: 4

ALL-TERRAIN VEHICLE

This vehicle is perfect for racing through busy traffic or narrow city streets to fight small fires.

Good for: putting out fires when no people are in danger, such as rubbish bins or blazing bonfires.
Kit on board: blue lights, first-aid kit, fire extinguisher and hoses.
Firefighters on board: 1

FIRE MOTORBIKE

THEORY 7

RESCUE VEHICLES

Whenever there is an emergency, firefighters have just the right vehicle for the job. As well as big trucks, they have more unusual ways to transport kit and crew, too.

Which vehicle would you choose for each of these emergencies?

○ Someone is trapped in sinking sand.
○ The forest is on fire.
○ A bonfire is out of control.

THEORY NO: 7
○ tick here
APPROVED

This robot is operated by remote control so firefighters can stay a safe distance from the flames while it sprays mist or foam.

Good for: fighting big fires that are too dangerous for firefighters to go near.
Kit on board: a powerful spray, plus a fan for clearing smoke and a big blade for clearing the way.
Firefighters on board: 0

FIRE ROBOT

This big truck can speed to fires far from smooth roads. Bumpy ground and rushing rivers are no problem for these giant tyres.

Good for: battling blazes in thick forests and steep mountainsides.
Kit on board: water and foam, hoses and pumps.
Firefighters on board: 3

OFF-ROAD TRUCK

This mini firefighter can race to road traffic accidents and give help before the big fire engines arrive.

Good for: weaving through queues on the motorway to put out car fires.
Kit on board: cutting equipment and medical kit.
Firefighters on board: 3

RAPID RESPONSE VEHICLE

An inflatable boat is used to reach people in trouble on rivers and lakes. It is towed on a trailer to wherever it is needed.

Good for: rescuing people caught in flooding.
Kit on board: life jackets, first-aid kit, blankets.
Firefighters on board: 2-4

RESCUE BOAT

WILDFIRE!

There's a fire burning in the forest and it's spreading fast! Fighting wildfires is tough, hot work, but luckily help is on hand from up above.

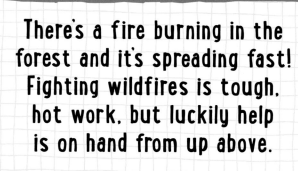

Special firefighters called 'smoke jumpers' parachute into hard-to-reach places.

WILDFIRE FORECAST

Check the weather below and decide if the fire risk is high or low.

1 Hot, dry weather dries out plants so that they catch fire easily.

2 Wind makes fire spread quickly and change direction without warning.

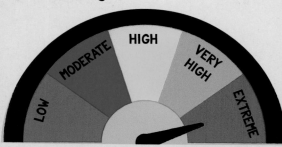

LOW   MODERATE   HIGH   VERY HIGH   EXTREME

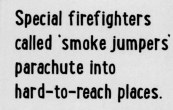

Firefighters carry waterpacks to hose the smouldering ground.

QUICK FIRE FACT
A fire plane can carry enough water to fill over 60 bath tubs!

A fire plane drops a tank of water on the fire below.

Helicopters hover overhead and drop water from giant buckets.

PRACTICAL NO: 10
tick here
APPROVED

A fire plane fills its tank by swooping low over a lake to scoop up water.

Bulldozers clear a path through the plants so that there is nothing for the fire to burn.

WILDFIRE TOOLS
Can you spot these tools being used?

○ Fire beater to smother the flames.
○ Axe to cut down trees that can burn.
○ Rake to scrape up dry twigs and leaves.

39

NATURAL DISASTERS

When disaster strikes, firefighters battle
through mud, wind, snow and ice
to keep us safe.

The damage: roads collapse and buildings fall down.

The job: firefighters put out fires and check for dangers. Broken gas pipes could cause an explosion.

EARTHQUAKES

FLOODS

The damage: rivers burst their banks and homes flood.

The job: firefighters launch boats to rescue people. They also deliver food and water to cut-off places.

✴ TRAINEE TIP

Work with other emergency workers to get the job done.
Make it safe for ambulance crews to reach injured people
and engineers to fix power cables.

BLIZZARDS

The damage: heavy snow and ice block roads.

The job: firefighters dig through deep drifts to reach people trapped in cars and homes.

HURRICANES

The damage: strong winds blow down trees and power lines.

The job: firefighters clear blocked roads and clean up debris.

THEORY NO: 8

◯ ⤴ tick here

⭐ APPROVED

ACTIVITY

Firefighters rescue people and animals who fall through thin ice. Can you find a route to the dog before he gets in trouble?

FLOATING AND FLYING

AIRPORTS

Airport firefighting teams race down runways to aircraft emergencies. They are specially trained to battle burning jet fuel.

Next time you're on a plane, listen to the air steward's instructions about emergencies.

O Special fire engines shoot jets of foam from a safe distance.

O A hose on a long mechanical arm can fight fires from above.

O Firefighters help passengers to escape from the plane safely.

TRAINEE TIP

Oil and fuel fires need to be put out with foam. Water makes the flames bigger!

Fires can start anywhere – even in the air or at sea.
Luckily, special crews are ready to answer every emergency.

AT SEA

Fireboats speed to fires on ships, oil rigs and on the shore. They suck up water from the sea, river or lake that they are floating on and blast it onto the blaze.

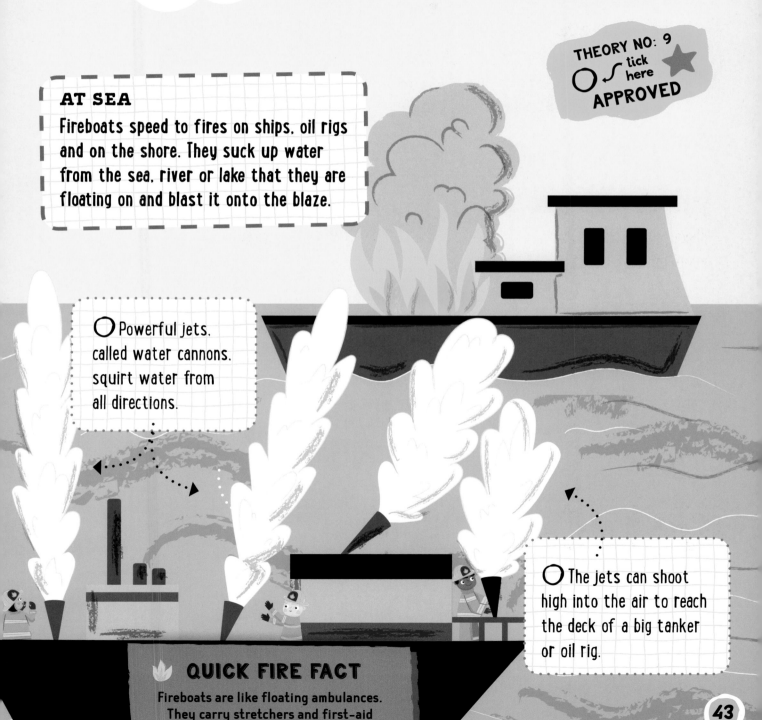

○ Powerful jets, called water cannons, squirt water from all directions.

○ The jets can shoot high into the air to reach the deck of a big tanker or oil rig.

🔥 QUICK FIRE FACT

Fireboats are like floating ambulances. They carry stretchers and first-aid kits for casualties.

EXAMINATION

Now it's time to see how much you have learned.

1 Which of these sentences is TRUE?

   a) Firefighters only fight fires.

   b) Firefighters don't just fight fires

2 What is the thing at the end of a fire hose called?

   a) A nuzzle

   b) A guzzle

   c) A nozzle

3 What are training sessions called?

   a) Bolts

   b) Drills

   c) Thrills

4 What does the pump on a fire engine do?

   a) Blows smoke away

   b) Blows up flat tyres

   c) Pushes water out of the hoses

5 What do smoke alarms do?

   a) Sprinkle water

   b) Spray smoke

   c) Beep loudly

6 What is a fire engine often called?

   a) The gadget

   b) The appliance

   c) The applause

7 Where do firefighters leave their boots?

   a) In the fire engine

   b) Under their bed

   c) Inside their trousers

8 What is a team of firefighters called?

   a) A watch

   b) A guard

   c) A wash

9 Why are dogs used by firefighters?

    a) They keep them company

    b) They have a good sense of smell

    c) They are good at climbing ladders

10 Which of these tools does a firefighter use most?

    a) Screwdriver

    b) Spanner

    c) Axe

11 Which type of emergency needs ropes and a harness?

    a) House fire

    b) Cliff rescue

    c) Road accident

12 Which of these is NOT real?

    a) Fire motorbike

    b) Fire robot

    c) Fire skateboard

13 Which of these sentences is FALSE?

    a) Fireplanes drop loads of water

    b) Fireplanes drop sand

14 What sort of weather causes wildfires?

    a) Warm and wet

    b) Hot and dry

    c) Cloudy and cold

FIRE SCORES

Check your answers at the back of the book and add up your score.

1 to 5 Alarm bells! Race back to the station and redo your training.

6 to 10 Hot stuff! You are on the ladder to becoming a great firefighter.

11 to 14 You're on fire! You really know your blaze-busting facts!

FIREFIGHTER SPEAK

aerial
Something that happens, moves or operates in the air.

apparatus
A machine, tool or piece of kit which has a special job to do.

casualty
A person who is injured or killed in an accident or war.

collapse
To crumble or fall down suddenly.

debris
Pieces from something that has been destroyed.

electric socket
A point on the wall where you can connect electrical equipment to the power supply.

fire extinguisher
A canister that contains water or foam to put out fires.

harness
Straps and belts used to hold a person or animal safely in place.

oxygen
The gas in the air that plants and animals need to live.

siren
A piece of equipment for making a loud warning noise.

smouldering
To burn slowly with smoke but no flames.

smother
To stop a fire by covering it with something that stops air from reaching it.

thermal
Something that saves, makes or detects heat.

turntable
A circular platform that can spin around.

FIREFIGHTER ACADEMY

WELL DONE!

You made it through your firefighter training.

Name...

FULLY QUALIFIED

FIREFIGHTER

ANSWERS

The things to find are circled to the side.

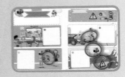

Page 9
Soak the flames with cold water or foam = take away heat

Cover the flames with something thick like a blanket = take away oxygen

Clear away plants and trees = take away fuel

Page 10–11
The answers are to the side.

Page 12–13
The things to find are circled to the side.

Page 13
The four differences are circled to the side.

Page 14–15
The things to find are circled below.

Page 16–17
The things are put away in the image below.

Page 20–21
1. Someone smelt smoke.
2. The information arrived at the fire station.
3. We put on protective gear and raced to the engine.
4. The driver talked to the control centre to get more information.
5. The engine sped through the streets.
6. Cars heard the siren and moved out of the way.
7. We arrived at the scene.
8. We entered the house.

Page 24
Firefighter Jack needs his tank topping up.

Page 29
You would need ropes, a harness and a hard hat for a rope rescue.

Page 31
The things to find are circled below.

Page 33
Restaurant = clean up the rubbish and keep the doorway clear

Bakery = keep extinguishers clear, clean and in working order

School = give the teachers posters to put up in the classroom

Homes = fit smoke alarms and show people how to check them

Page 34–35
The things to spot are circled to the side.

Page 36–37
Sinking sand = all-terrain vehicle
Forest fire = off-road
Bonfire out of control = fire motorbike

Page 38–39
The things to find are circled below.

Page 41
The solution to the maze is to the side.

Page 44
1 = b; 2 = c; 3 = b; 4 = c; 5 = c;
6 = b; 7 = c; 8 = a; 9 = b; 10 = c;
11 = b; 12 = c; 13 = b; 14 = b.